GOODNIGHT ZOMBIE

Written by Morgan Duran
Illustrated by Teja Arboleda

www.EntertainingDiversity.com

Written by Morgan Duran
Illustrated by Teja Arboleda

Entertaining Diversity Press is a subsidiary of
Entertaining Diversity, Inc.

ISBN-13: 978-0692760192
ISBN-10: 0692760199

This book is dedicated to all the children who believe in Santa Claus, The Easter Bunny, The Tooth Fairy and unicorns.

In the bloodstained room

There was a bat

And a broken broom

And a zombie that –

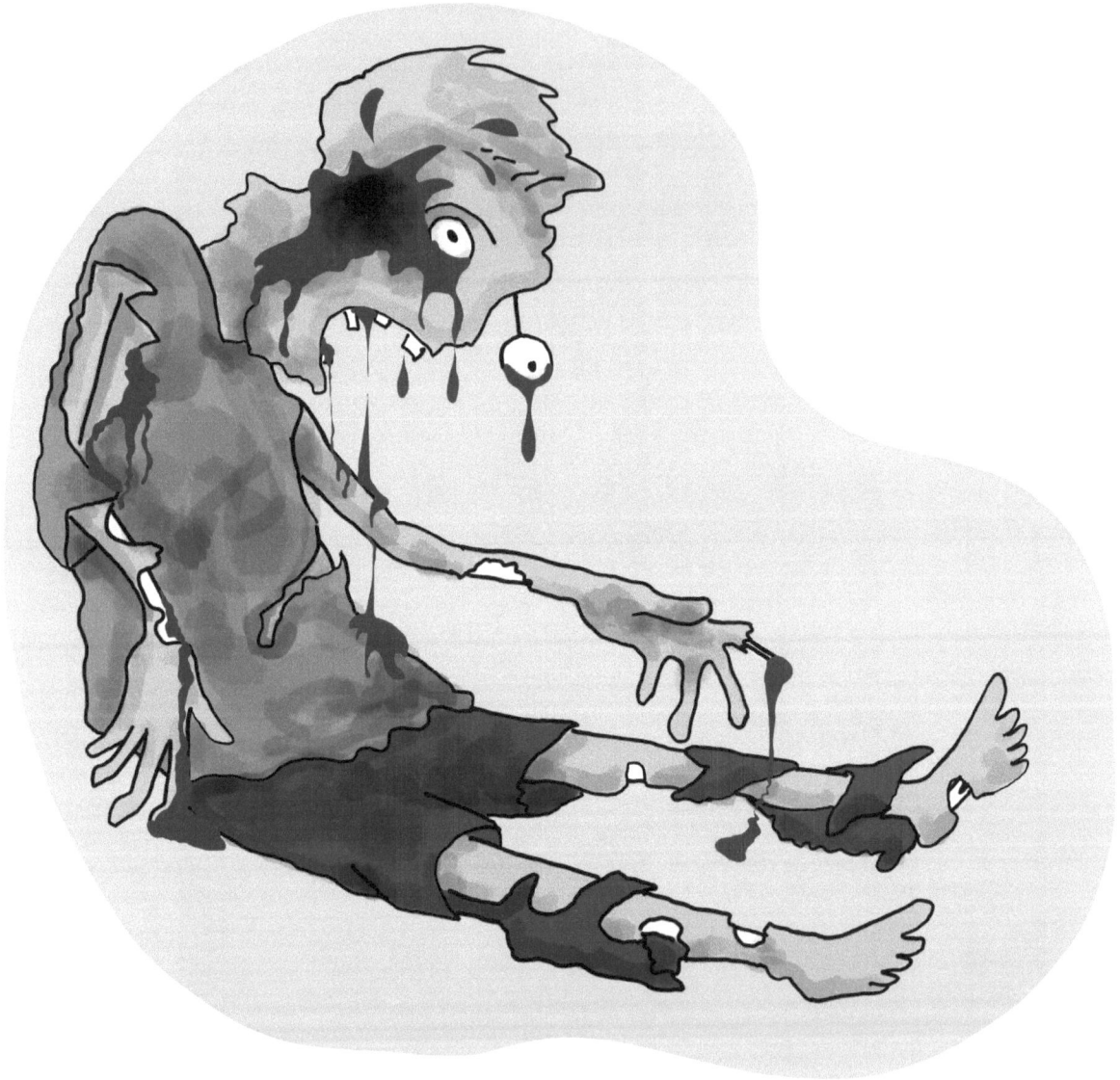

Smelled just like mushroom

And there were pieces of skin and a dead grin

And a half-eaten brain
That used to be Jane

And a machete that cuts
And a pile of wet guts

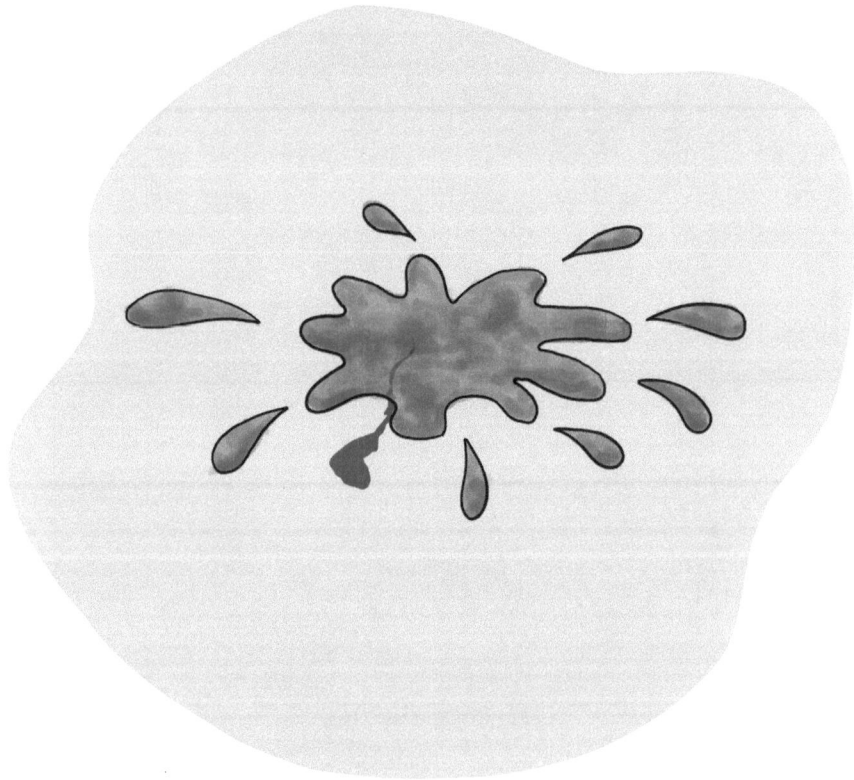

And a splatter of drool that looked just like gruel

And a limp tied-up postman bit all the way through

Goodnight room

Goodnight zombie

Who smelled like mushroom

Goodnight bat
Goodnight broken brain

Goodnight skin
Goodnight grin

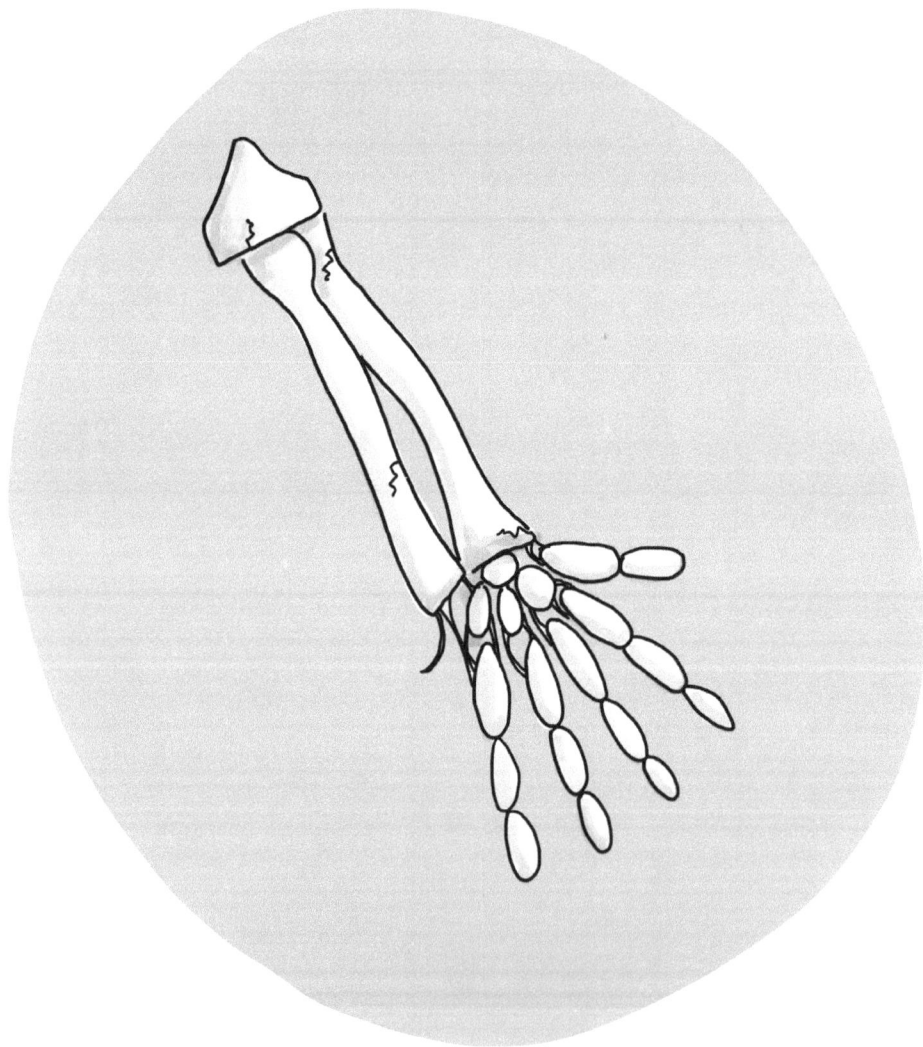

Goodnight bone

Goodnight phone

Goodnight eyeball
And goodnight broken skull

Goodnight blade that cuts

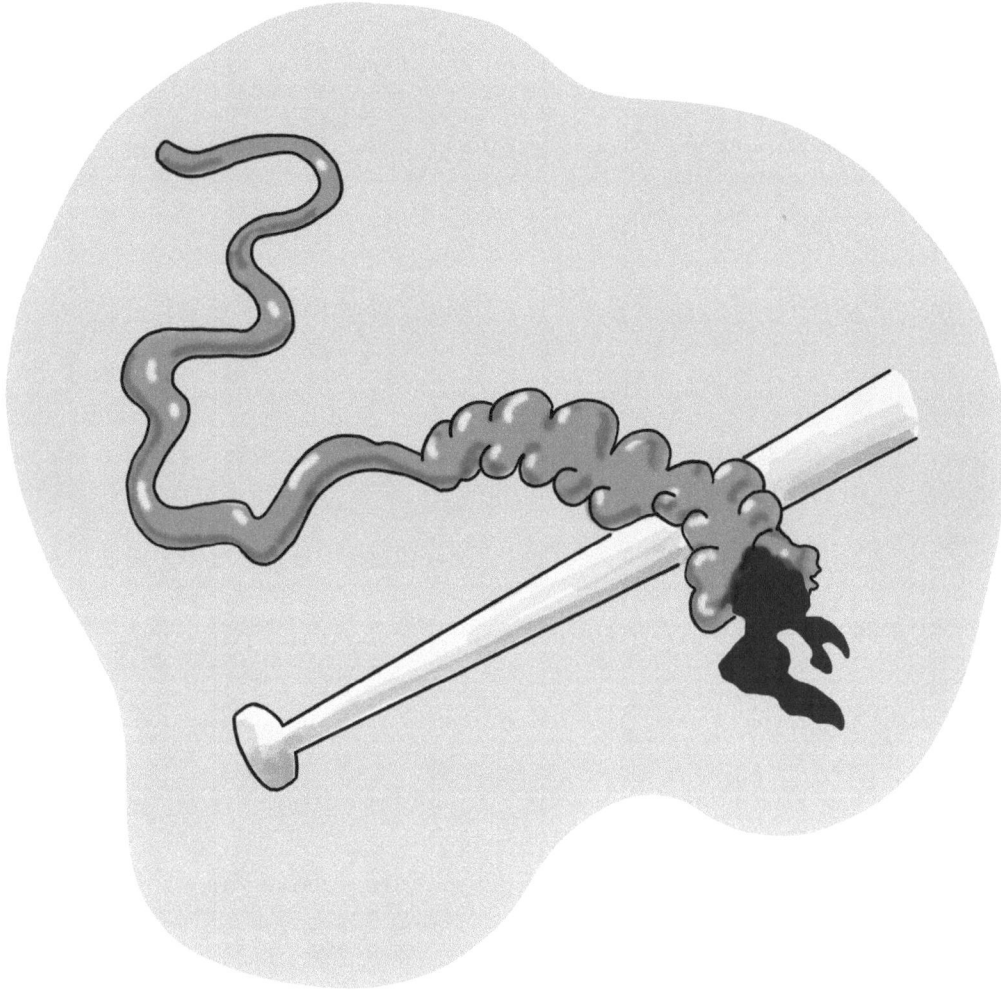

And goodnight wet guts

Goodnight latte
And goodnight mouse

Goodnight ramen

Goodnight house

And goodnight postman
bit all the way through

Goodnight doll

Goodnight nightmare

Goodnight undead everywhere

Do not try this at home.

About The Author

Morgan lives in the Boston area with her husband, daughter and two cats. She is an enthusiastic geek with a passion for technology, science fiction, Doctor Who, Stephen King and anything associated with Joss Whedon.

About The Illustrator

Teja is a television producer, professor, illustrator, writer and geek, and would not like his brain to be eaten.

www.ingramcontent.com/pod-product-compliance
Lightning Source LLC
Chambersburg PA
CBHW042104040426
42448CB00002B/138